SPECIMEN POSTE

des

CARACTÈRES EN BOIS

de la Maison

Bonnet & Cᵒ

 PARIS

First Published in August 2019
First Edition

Gingko Press, Inc.
2332 Fourth Street, Suite E
Berkeley, CA 94710, USA
email: books@gingkopress.com

Gingko Press Verlags GmbH
Schulterblatt 58
20357 Hamburg, Germany
email: gingkopress@t-online.de

www.gingkopress.com

ISBN: 978-1-58423-266-7

Printed in Lithuania.

Typography in Wood

WOOD TYPOGRAPHY FROM THE 19TH CENTURY

GINGKO PRESS

TA Grand CHARENE

MANAis NAPOL

MAma BUA

CARa MU

METr

REa KY

Ma

Introduction

BY MARTINE COTREL

»Specimen des caractères en bois [Wood Type Specimens] de la maison Bonnet« is a mail order catalog from a Parisian manufacturer of wooden characters and »other printing materials« found in an exceptional state of preservation in the collections of the Bibliothèque des arts graphiques, à Paris. Founded by typographer Edmond Morin (1859-1937) and donated to the City in 1919, this library is rich with about 30,000 documents (books and journals) devoted to printing, typography and various printmaking techniques. It also has a collection of about 800 specimens of typographical characters also called booklets. The largest French and foreign foundries from the years 1860-1960 (Mayeur, Turlot, Deberny and Peignot, Schelter and Giesecke, etc.) are represented. Now accessible to the public via the Forney Library in Paris, this rare collection remained abandoned for several years, and some important books have degraded in condition. Catalog Bonnet is the exception that proves the rule: quality poster paper used for

this edition has hitherto been preserved without alteration. It has been precisely analyzed by the French author Michel Wlassikoff, who mentioned that »this catalog probably dates from the 1860s – a period when Romantic phantasmagoria was on the decline in the structure of the letter but still prevalent in its outlines; type design was beginning to borrow from the architectural eclecticism of the age, and sometimes resembled wrought ironwork. In addition to dated products, series of surprisingly ›modern‹ types were developed that could, somewhat ironically, be compared with those generated by the ›new‹ digital typography. The republication of this catalog demonstrates that letters, like buildings, incarnate the spirit of an age, while preserving a timeless quality that constitutes a lasting source of inspiration«.

Martine Cotrel
Former Curator of Bibliothèque des arts graphiques, Paris

Foreword

BY CHRISTIAN ACKER

This book is not just a collection of bygone but exquisite and unexpected alphabets. It's a time capsule of a period between the classical and modern periods of design and thought.

Typography and design are fascinating windows into understanding the shifts of history. So much of the technological advancements, shared values and worldview of a given time and place can be seen in those curves, counters, stems and serifs. If you knew nothing of the history of the 19th Century and came across this collection of Parisian type specimens you might be struck by how bold, contemporary and varied the forms were. Some are spartan and simple, others exude confident flourish or blunt force in their shapes and counters. Some are brash with exploding dimension. But they are all fighting for your attention, with more respect for personality and style than quiet finesse. None here act coy. And that was a shift from the age that preceded it, where printing innovation was mostly confined to books and texts of more consid-erable length and smaller size. And that shift was a shift not just in technology but in thought.

The 19th Century saw a new era of broader trade and commerce. Industrialization started the commercial age we now find our-selves in (up to our necks and rising swiftly by the day it seems). Before planned obsolescence and seasonal color stories merchants had the need of calling for your attention on busy city streets where signs and placards were the analog though primary communication tools available. This development demanded new typographic forms of a more expressive nature. Shopkeepers and snake oil salesmen alike knew emotional connection in messaging was more effective than clarity – long before David Carson advised us »don't confuse legibility with communication.« As we settle deeper and more comfortably into our post-modern age, it is not just beauty that is found in the eye of the beholder, but meaning itself is now the responsibility of the audience as well.

In a few short seasons, design tastes can change and our impressions of the meaning associated with those aesthetics shift too. A typeface like any style can fall in or out of favor – even changing its meaning by association to its message.

Typography is the visual equivalent of the accent or sound of a spoken language. When looking at language, it is a fascinating observation that the polyglot who has mastered multiple tongues can not only converse fluently with those of different cultures, but also has their own thinking altered by the use of a different language. Multi-linguists become more sympathetic not only to their conversational partners but can understand their thoughts, motivations and world view more fully when speaking their language. Nelson Mandela once observed, »If you talk to a man in a language he understands, that goes to his head. If you talk to him in his language, that goes to his heart.« The more refined and acute a communication technology becomes the more subtle or varied its content can become, allowing aesthetics to influence the perception and reception of a message.

Not all messages are meant for all mediums and vice versa. Entire organizing mental structures have changed alongside our shifts in cultural values and technologies. What took thousands of years to establish, took only the last 500 or so to change drastically – and more and more drastically in the few generations that saw the 20th and start of the 21st century. Ancient antiquity's ideas of geometric proportion, balance and beauty epitomized in the golden ratio necessitate a path – not just for the eye in a composition but for the mind in a story. But as industrialization became the norm and matrix of our world we have seen a move from an organizing structure based upon Phi, to the short hand of a grid based upon thirds, then shifting again most recently to a new grid based upon equidistant cubic squares.

Our modern mental structure is a grid resembling the board game Battleship. Plot your points. Shoot in the dark. Create understanding based upon the hits and misses, not the unwinding arc of storyline, as was the modus operandi of ancient and more homogenous cultures. As technology progressed to machines with interchangeable parts we see an infinitely customizable future – contributing to our means and desire to be more expressive and more individual while creating a more cluttered media environment. In our quest to plot points we mimic stock market charts and progressive social politics which both tell us a story of ever increasing progress. These charts have ups and downs, but they always move onward and upward. Not a spiraling out like the ancient Fibonacci sequence.

The appeal of these pre-modern wooden type forms in a post-modern digital age is that they are representative of a transitional period between an ancient and a modern world. We are currently finding ourselves in a similar but newly disillusioned transition period. Modern progressive thought rejected the long unwinding of history for the hope of an ever-upward line of impersonal progress. Post–modernism became disillusioned with this story in its oversimplification. But our lives are now entrenched in this world of hacked grid works and confused proportions. Cutting through the clutter to reach more audience is no longer viable. Cutting through the clutter to reach your audience is now key. And authenticity is the buzzword of the moment as we seek to connect person to person again. The type in this book is evidence of a human hand. It has a hint of industriousness yet is not quite industrial. It is interchangeable without being replaceable. It may be our opportunity to discover a way forward. How great is it that we can see those personal and human values and view of the world in the curves, counters, stems and serifs of letters carved from wood in a bygone era? If we can see it here, can we see it everywhere? Can we learn to see it in our own time? Or will it take a hundred years and another generation to see the shifts, changes and values embedded in our grids, curves, counters, stems and serifs? I have no answers yet, I'm just starting to plot the positions of the battle ships as I seek understanding of where it is we came from in order to plot a course forward.

Christian Acker
Creative Director, designer and author. Founder of Adnauseum.

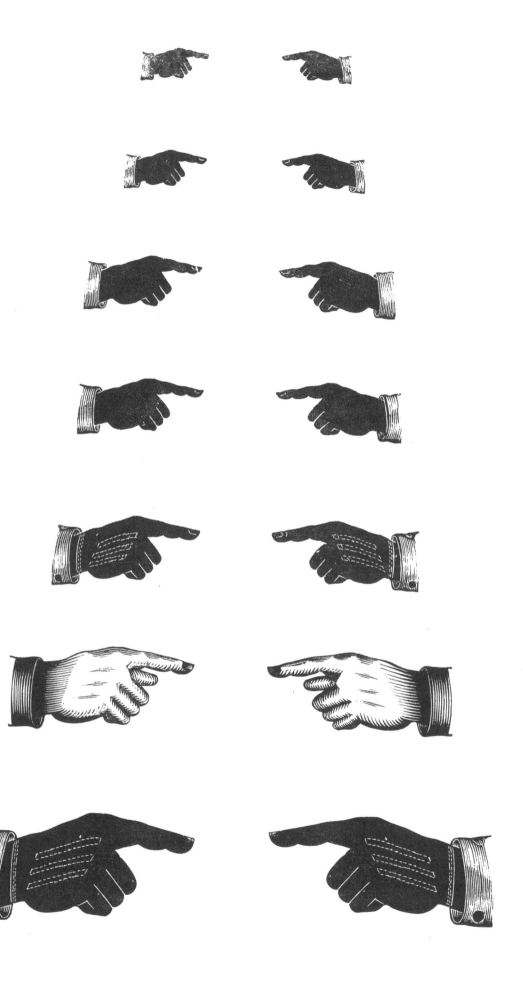

SAMPLE SECTION

no. **1**

NATION Sesam

CADRE Vitas

NOTE Seal

ARE Gar

EIS Ba

ARa

ENe

GIE

no. **2**

DEO Afra | ART Set

BE La | SERie

ERu | Tir

Ee | Ki

no. **3**

SPECIMEN POSTE DES CARACTÈRES EN BOIS DE LA MAISON BONNET & CO.

14

EUR 13

FUT

Rer

CH

Eu

EI

E

H

A

E

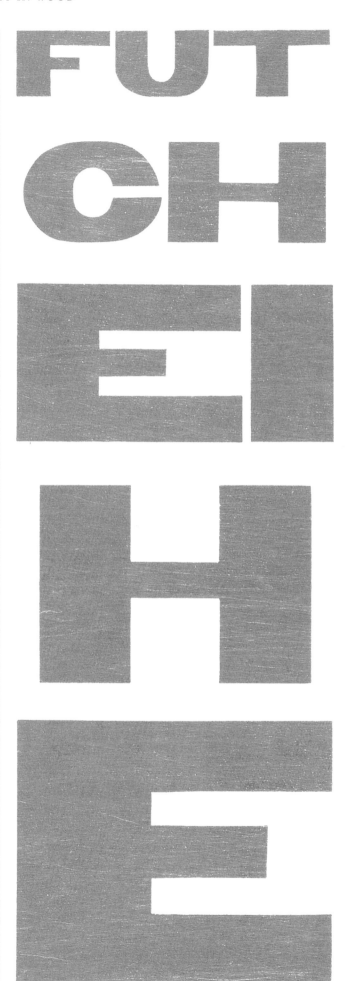

no. **4**

SPECIMEN POSTE DES CARACTÈRES EN BOIS DE LA MAISON BONNET & CO.

CARACTERES | RIO Nouvelle

CHATEL | ORSort

EURIA | ERno

AR | A5

no. **5**

FONTE | HORST
TON ERL
RE BA
FER DESEPOQUE
EL GARE
FI! CROC

no. **6**

DEUS Rennes

OR Cordia

SIR Cire

BA Rai

ROS

EXCELLE

Nation 50

AMDEN

Réseda

GARE

Babel

LEO

Sara

no. **7**

SPECIMEN POSTE DES CARACTÈRES EN BOIS DE LA MAISON BONNET & CO.

BARDE Xylographie

PLEA Nero 2

CRAZ Sir

GIN Liar

BIRn

TIBER Sola

AR Gais

ODer 7

CISia

ELa

no. **8**

GERB Prote 2 | REVU Niel

TINE Adier SE Len

LOT Car EO Pa

GERe SLet

JURe ESSe

BRa Sie

no. **9**

SPECIMEN POSTE DES CARACTÈRES EN BOIS DE LA MAISON BONNET & CO.

26

MANCHE NAIC 12
BEX ANC2
GER CAN
EZ2 NE
KY N1
ES N

no. **10**

SPECIMEN POSTE DES CARACTÈRES EN BOIS DE LA MAISON BONNET & CO.

BRILLE ODEN
NIERS PER
TRIK NUI
ZR5 HN
OS B
GU E

no. **11**

SPECIMEN POSTE DES CARACTÈRES EN BOIS DE LA MAISON BONNET & CO.

30

Pair
ERa
San
Ma
Ar
Ai
R

ENa
Ma
Na
Ae
R
H
R

no. **12**

AU MOULIN FRAGILE

LES MULATRES DE

DE LA FRANCE

L'ASCENSION

POPULAIRE

NATIONAL Phila

DANCE Race DE

HUSS Typo 2

REY Gast

MEKA

no. **13**

PARME Bern 2

PEINE BUG

MAP Lira 6

RIO Sat

LAR Suez

BEL 38

O Gra

Bah

AEca

N U

no. **14**

BONHEUR

ARN Sar 2

BONDER

BE Rath

DEBEC

NOIRe

DORF

Ars

HOE

NEa

DEC

Aar

no. **15**

HISTOIRE MORALE
SOLDA ANGE
ARIE URF
ARC EIS
AL ES
RS TI

no. **16**

PORTIS TOM 7

CALC Reb

BOK Can

AL Bm

RE Go

ES Ri

no. **17**

NEW
AIN
RI
D
B
E

ROG-
M
E
B
R
E

no. **18**

MEIN Arte

RArem

Calvin

ENne

ROa

SAn

Hn

no. **19**

RAPHALisea CARLTaten2

PERLSam RECTGro

ROLnoa EROisa

MEIsr RSoe

ARa NIa

no. **20**

SPECIMEN POSTE DES CARACTÈRES EN BOIS DE LA MAISON BONNET & CO.

48

PUFNocane | BAGrad

RYESmo | RAZIm

SITEa | MAea

ASm | Mari

Arit | Eda

Ea | Ea

no. **21**

EArt

BHis

Me2

En3

EH

Ae

Ce

NE

HE

ET

M

E

B

J

no. **22**

HERD Ems KPar
ASPEGrot Ghel
MAPOst Mei
ENRue B5
NLia7 Oi

no. **23**

RORSCHACH RADETSkil

SCHWEIZER SHOPEis

MENAGE LADone

FORIA ALEa

ALPE GAta

GAN SEa

no. **24**

DELEMONT
BISSON 13
KEBCL
SADUS
GITE
CAB

no. **25**

STAME er

MAN the

OFFICE

GINalt

ARm

He

GREEN OR

BELLERS

REMARK

ADMIT

TUDE

SET

no. **26**

SELMa

JEUDe

MAi

SAr

SIr

Ge

OUTCar

HEma

FLot

Hai

En

E

no. **27**

GENESIS Citorel OIE

TOURS Hair SEG

HEROLD Tart

TIGE Porte

DOUX En

CReUS

Duo

no. **28**

RAISON Elia 53

LE Moment

PORC Dent

GIO Poir

PEIne

SEa

Hit

no. **29**

SPECIMEN POSTE DES CARACTÈRES EN BOIS DE LA MAISON BONNET & CO.

JOLI DUO DU

SEN HON

BURGEN

GOSTIL

KENT

RYDE

HEIM

GER

OR

BC

no. **30**

RHOE
HEG
UB
HI
R

AUGARTEN
ARCHITE
HIOBE
REPT
QUI

no. **31**

MEKHEIM
GEMEINE
VERIE
TENK
ROSE
GIE

DO
U

no. **32**

NAVAL Chea 38 NURIO Pélicerie

LAC Ivresse LINE Rhin

DICT Mai TORome

MAman SERa 6

PisaH ROT

no. **33**

Ormeaux
LIST Art
PRAna
GENT

no. **34**

GIRAmi 45

MOSNac

ROSEN

REUE

LEO

MELONS

BERG

BUK

WU

XU

no. **35**

MESSAGER | MARKOS

HERTA | PEDRO

SALUC | MAR

SER | AN

HE | ED

no. **36**

EISRea

HOLa

REal

Boa

AP

MAILS

REIM

TEN

UR

IM

no. **37**

no. **38**

no. **39**

VASSER

OSA

EMESA

RN

BADE

DE

PAR

no. **40**

SPECIMEN POSTE DES CARACTÈRES EN BOIS DE LA MAISON BONNET & CO.

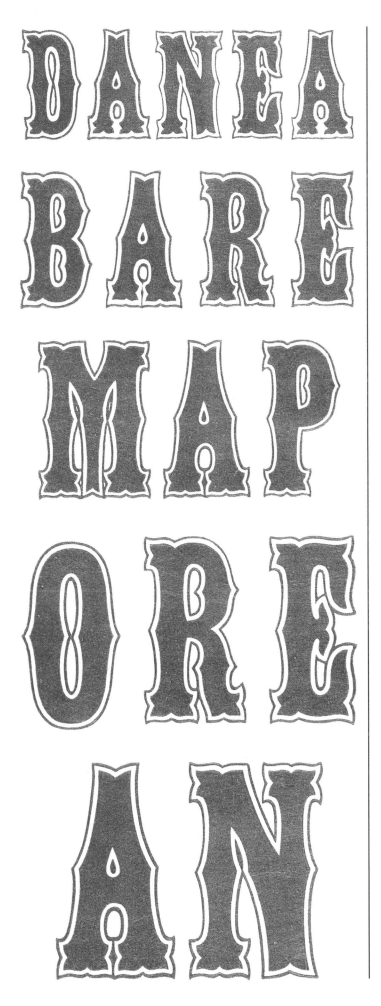

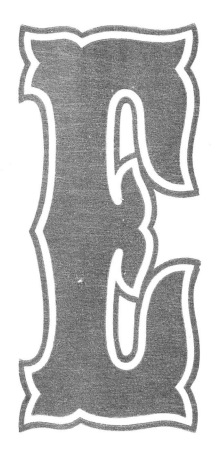

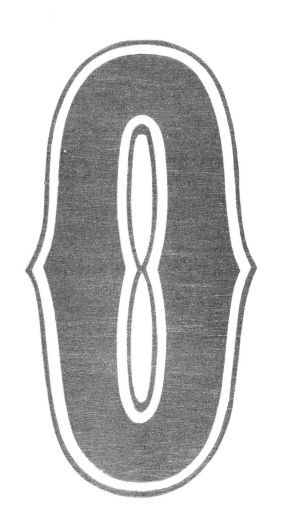

no. **41**

TA Grand

MANAis

MAma

CARa

METr

REa

Ma

CHARENE

NAPOL

BUA

MU

KY

no. **42**

MARIN

DROC

MUR

MU

EIS

no. **43**

JOUETS ANEtru
TOPSU SUtra
JUPE Nat
TUT LOI
NU EU
JE OS

no. **44**

no. **45**

RALSEUS

MARIN

FERE

RUE

VAR

no. **46**

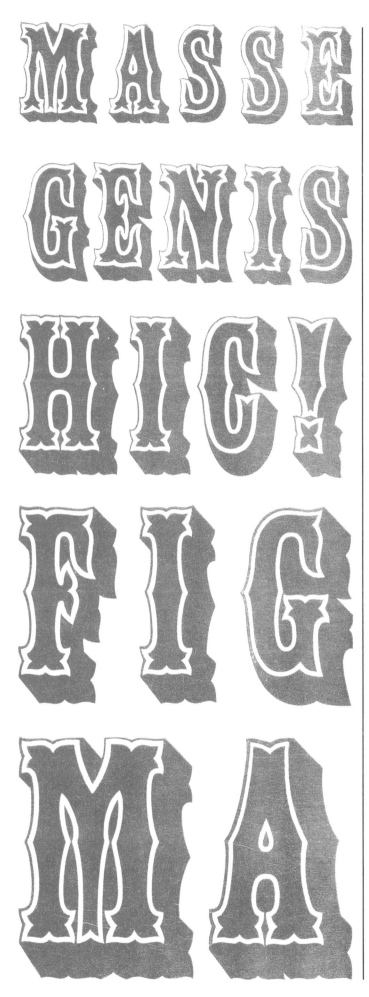

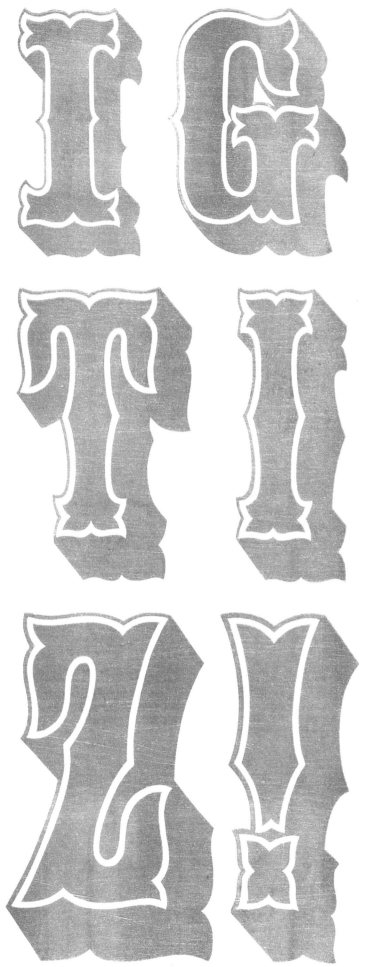

no. **47**

no. **48**

BARTO
PERD
RAF
ROI
BE

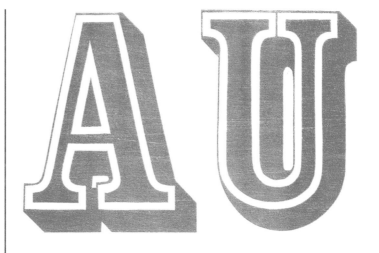

AU
H
N

no. **49**

MAC he
GAma
Vaud
UCo
Dul

Si
U

no. **50**

no. **51**

SANDO

Tam

SEN

Noh

AN

Lor

RU

DE

OI

Ut

no. **52**

TRAVAIL

MARCS

FERNI

NER

GAR

no. **53**

MARDI

CAR

OR

D!

no. **54**

MASSE
GENIS
HIC!
GIF
MA

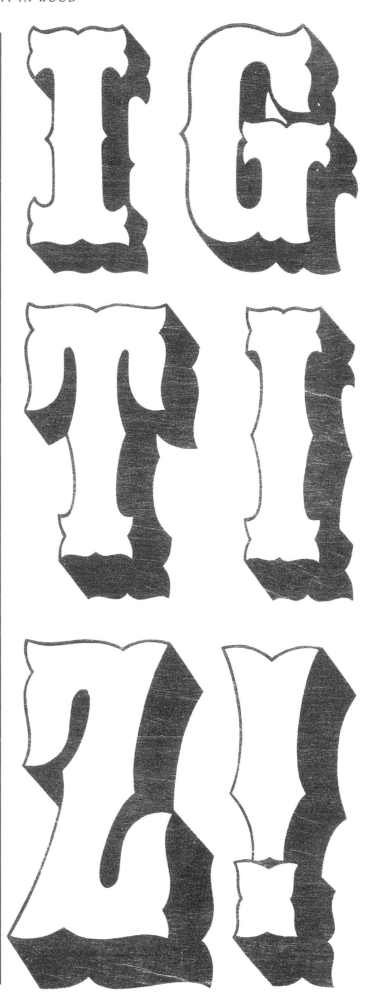

no. **55**

MOSEL
PERD
FAR
RIO
BA

AU
IJ
E

no. **56**

no. **57**

JOTa
BHo
LIIa
DU
Er

R
Sa
F

no. **58**

GESIMA
SULFA
PHAR
VAO
MA
CEP

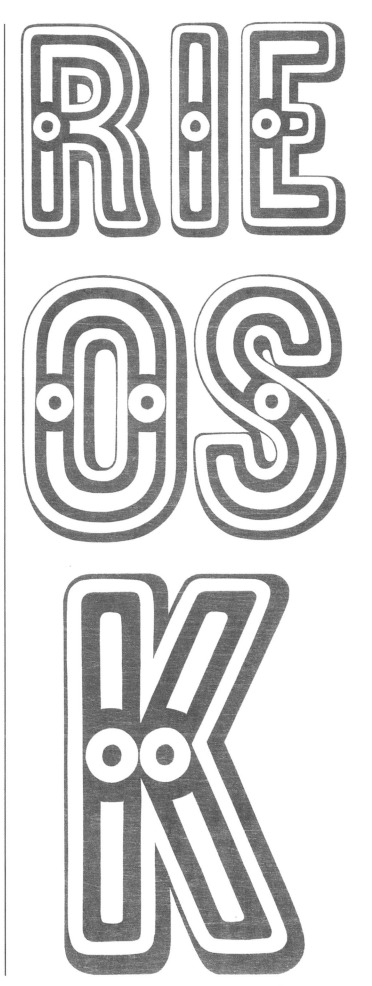

RIE
OS
K

no. **59**

A T U

M E

E R

M

G T U

G R E C E

R U X

B A S

R U

no. **60**

no. **61**

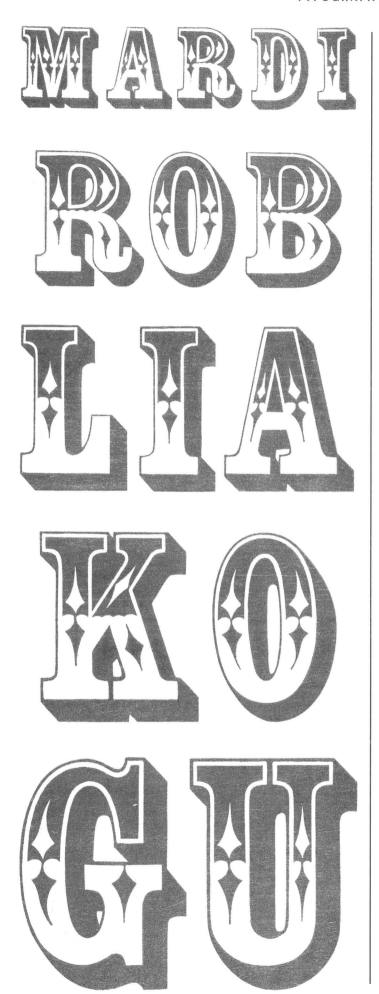

no. **62**

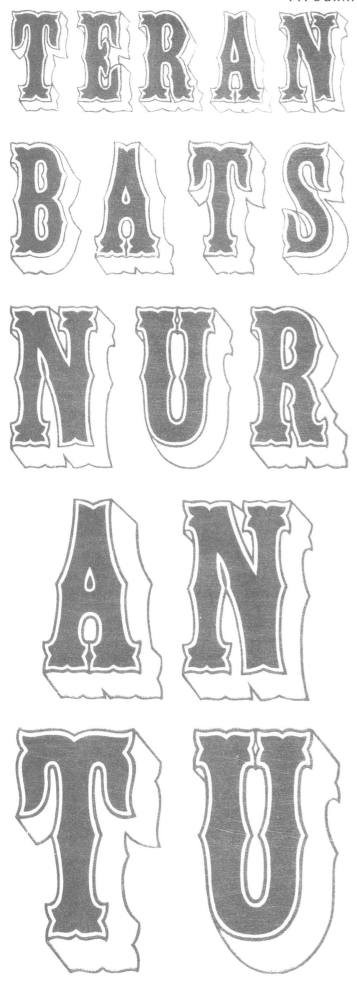

no. **63**

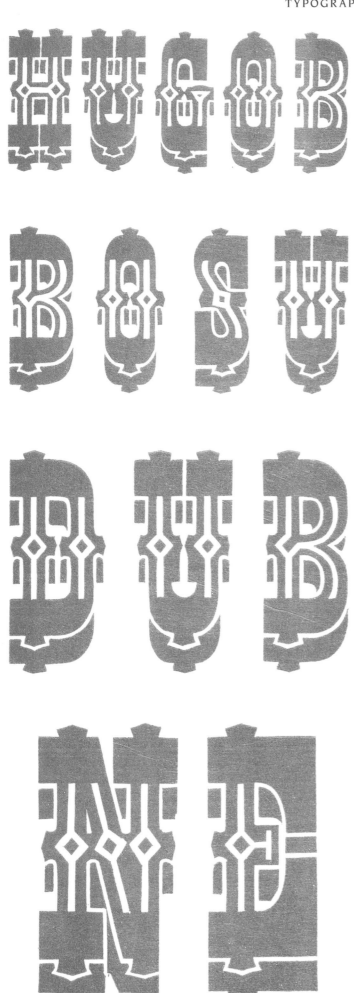

no. **64**

FEIL

AUS

RIE

GENS

AIX

PERN

SER

R

no. **65**

SPECIMEN POSTE DES CARACTÈRES EN BOIS DE LA MAISON BONNET & CO.

אבגהוזחט

יכלמנסעפ

צקרשתםן

ךףץ ∴

אבגהוזחט

no. **66**

RABELAIS £
Californie !

BRUNS £
Glascov

DORSE
bachel

HEND

SIMO
UTO
lade
RE

no. **67**

SPECIMEN POSTE DES CARACTÈRES EN BOIS DE LA MAISON BONNET & CO.

142

G A R E
P e s N
R O M
F a 4 2
M 6 3
I A 3

H 2 2
I L
E

no. **68**

GAZEH
Bedous

MOIR
Bieg7

BR 3
Erm
AH!

Ne5
HU
SL
Ik

no. **69**

SPECIMEN POSTE DES CARACTÈRES EN BOIS DE LA MAISON BONNET & CO.

MARTHA
Waes £26

ROCHE
Sorame

BASLE

AGIO

ROM
AM
A
ER
E
M
R

no. **70**

KIEL
Roma
CAP
May
OIL
E T
S W

NEWS

no. **71**

RACE
GLOB
SEA
RIO
RE
E3
EI

K
H
I!

no. **72**

no. **73**

TROCHU
Die Boch

BOW

EIDOH
Parise

DIN

ERIA
The U

Are

SIR

U£

no. **74**

BORSA

MEISE

ROE4

BEN

RIE

NB

E5

M

R

no. **75**

NAPLES !

WIEN 37

MARI

MER

MIS

BM

HE
E2
D

no. **76**

LE RITAN | SHOLD 72
MIS 25 | RUINE
GUAK | PATE
PER | NICE
NE | ES4
BU | RI

no. **77**

SPECIMEN POSTE DES CARACTÈRES EN BOIS DE LA MAISON BONNET & CO.

162

no. **78**

no. **79**

Muri
ZRd
Aal
Fh
Eb

Ca
IS
G

no. **80**

no. **81**

no. **82**

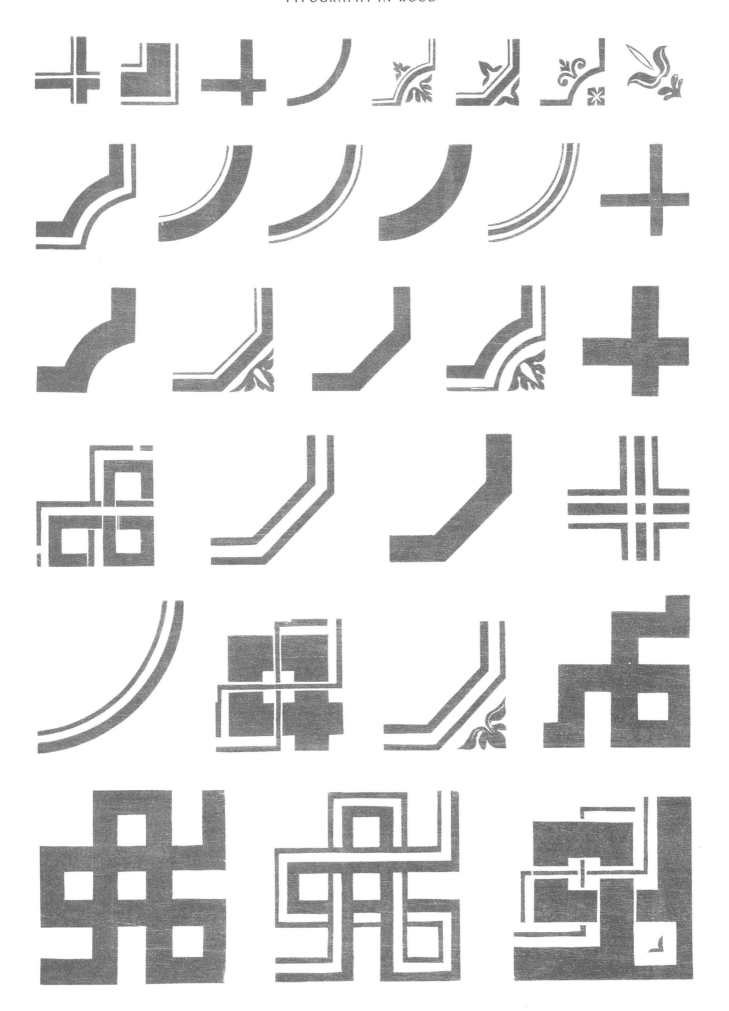

no. **83**

no. **84**

no. **85**

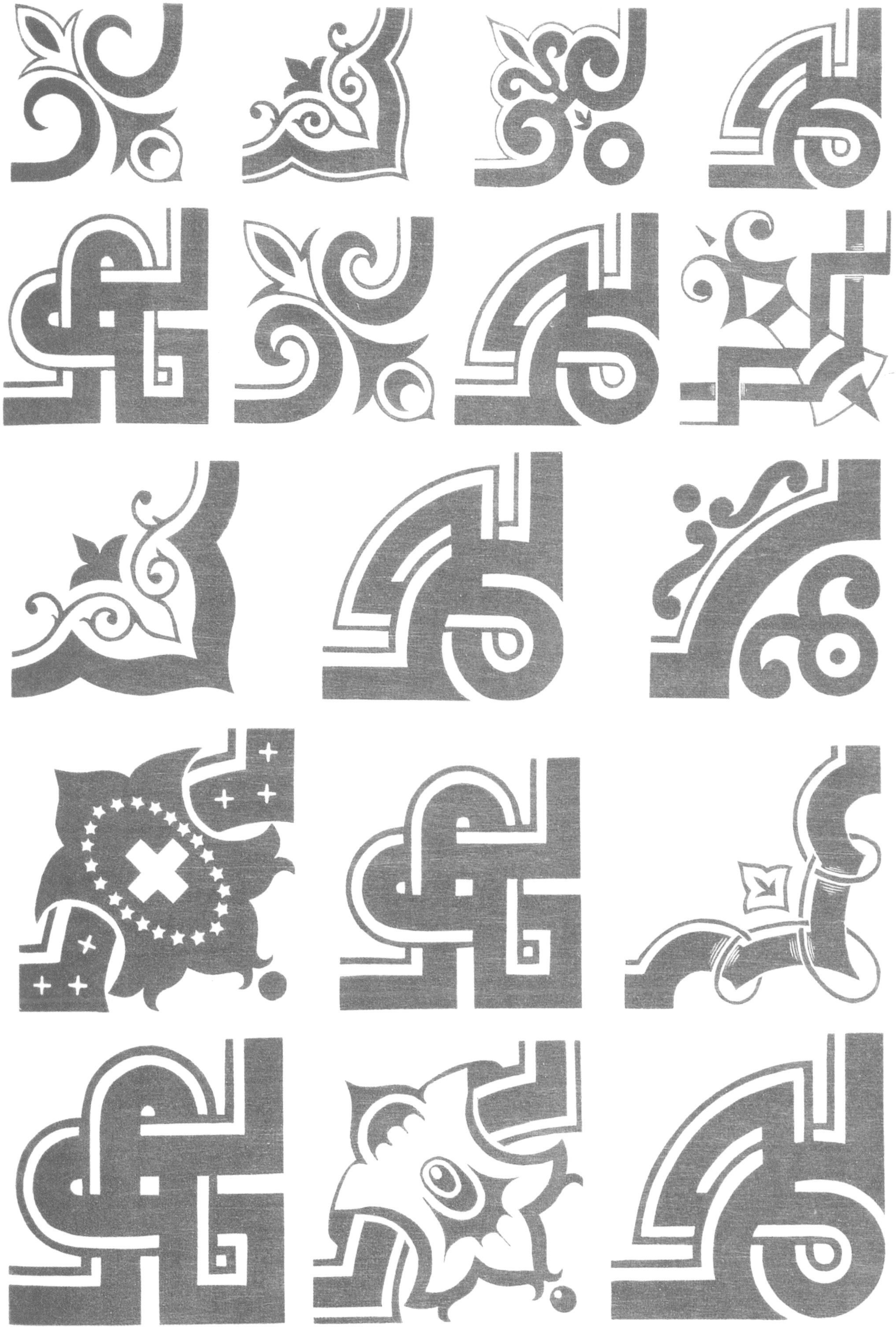

no. **86**

no. **87**

no. **88**

no. **89**

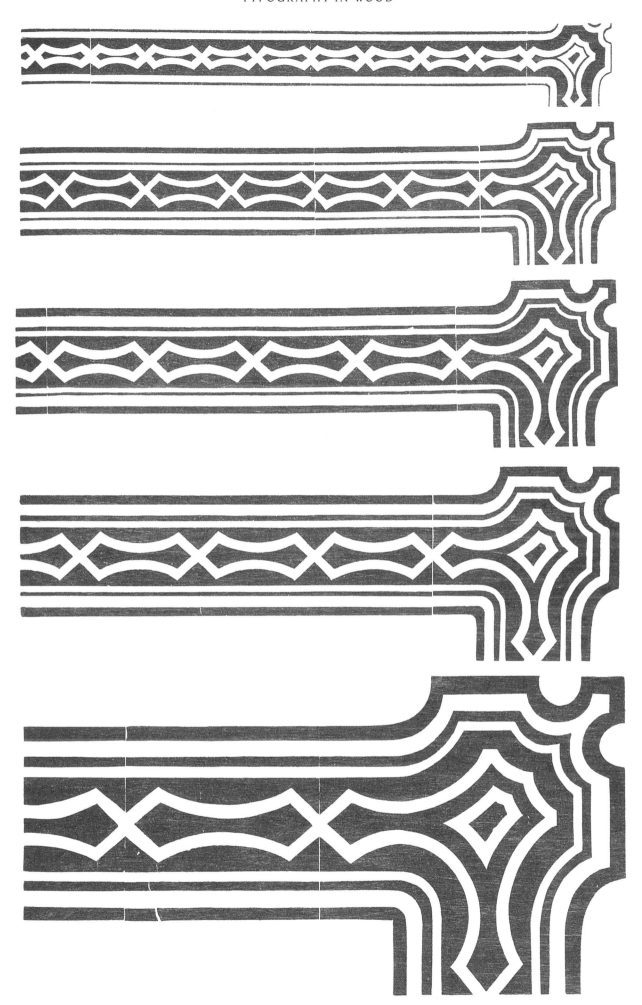

no. **90**

no. **91**

no. **92**

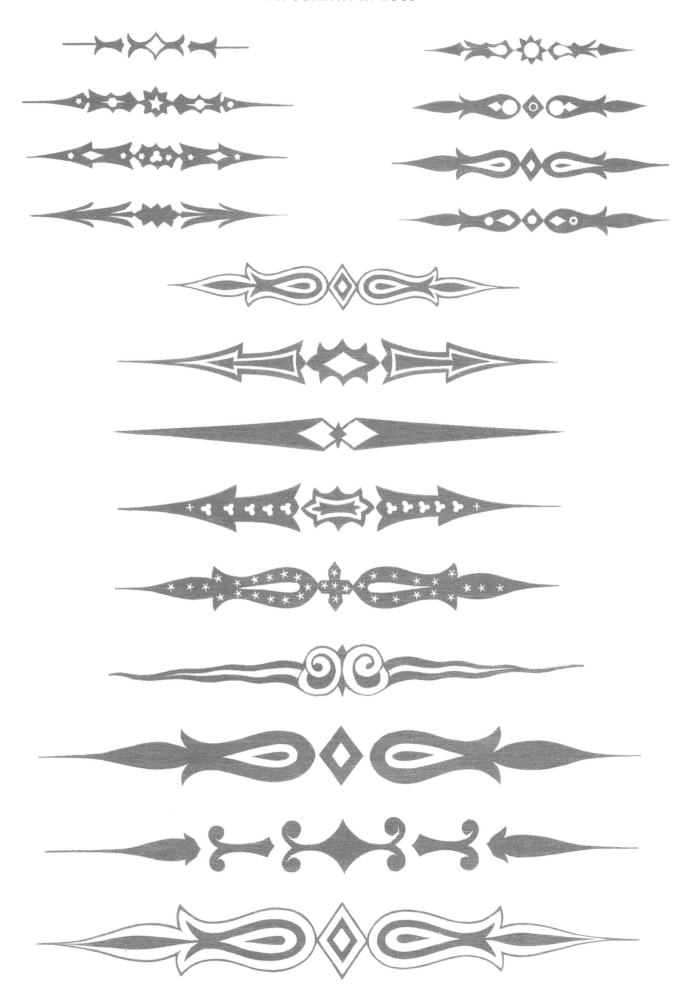

no. **93**

no. **94**

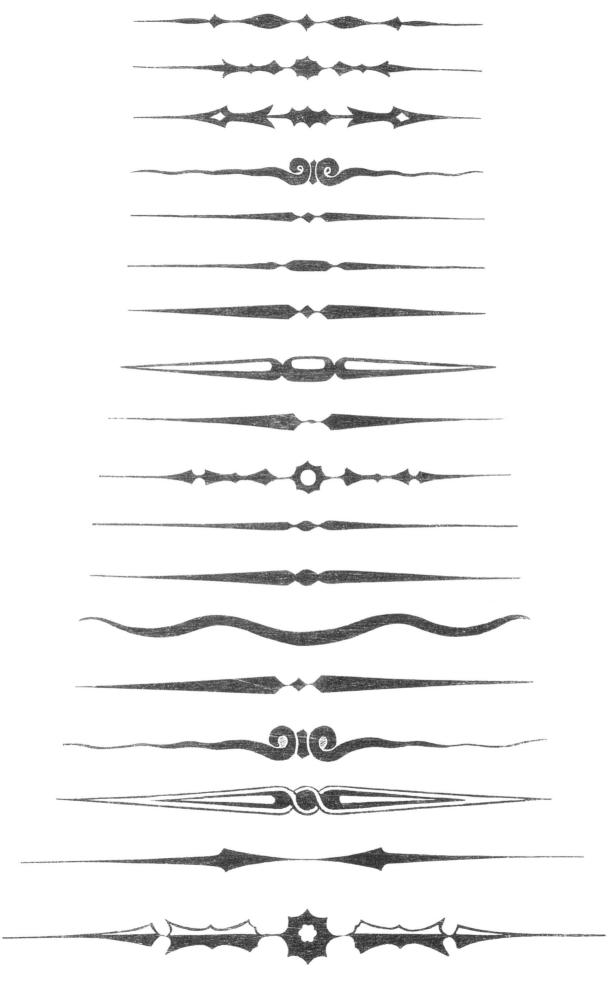

no. **95**

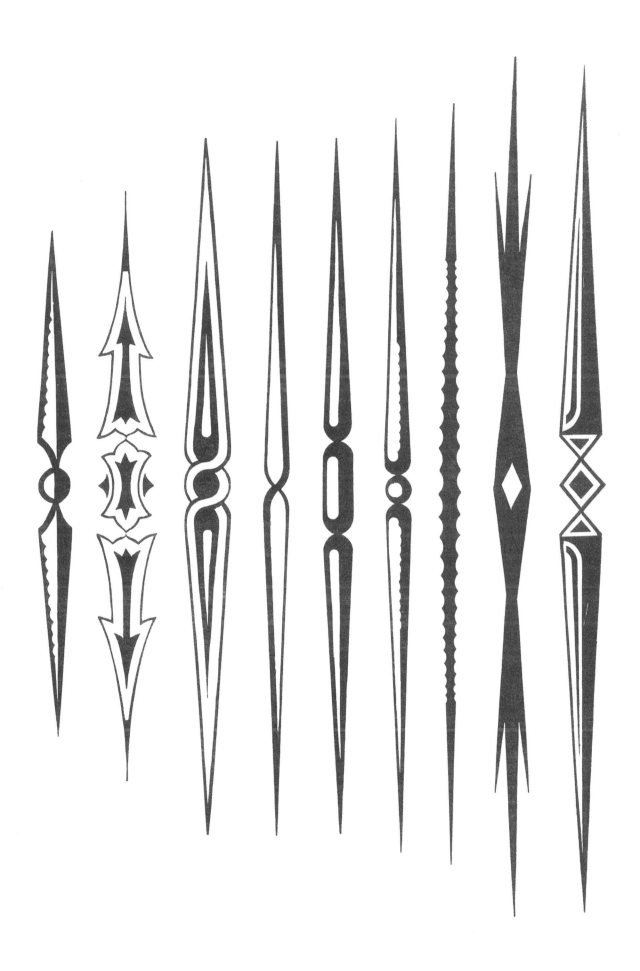

no. **96**

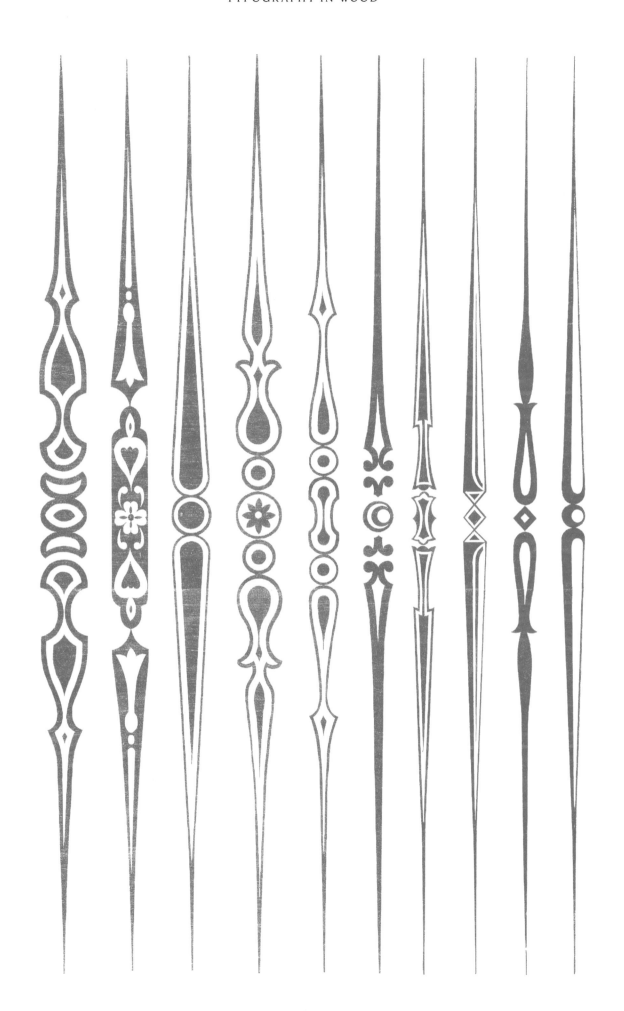

no. **97**

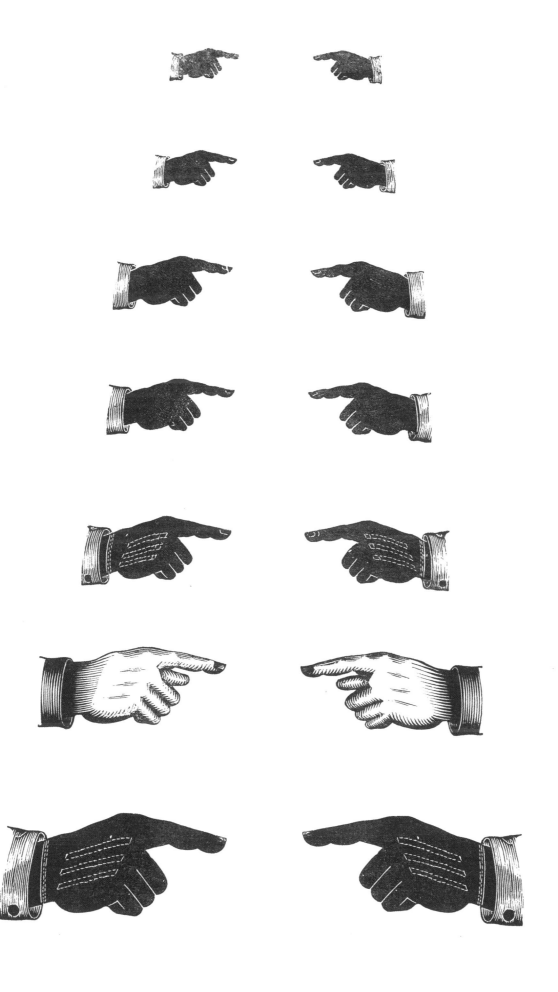